IMAGES
of America

SANTA ROSA COUNTY

This bridge crosses Pond Creek where Juan de la Rua built a dam in 1817 to power a sawmill. The town of Arcadia grew up around it and included a bucket factory and silk cocoonery. When Joseph Forsyth moved the mill operations to Bagdad around 1840, the old mill was converted to a cotton factory run by female slaves. The dam was blown up during the Civil War and never rebuilt. Arcadia is now a 34-acre historical nature park maintained by the Santa Rosa Historical Society and is located just west of Milton, off Highway 90.

IMAGES of America
SANTA ROSA COUNTY

Laurie Green

Copyright © 1998 by Laurie Green
ISBN 978-1-5316-3344-8

Published by Arcadia Publishing
Charleston, South Carolina

Library of Congress Catalog Card Number: Applied for

For all general information contact Arcadia Publishing at:
Telephone 843-853-2070
Fax 843-853-0044
E-mail sales@arcadiapublishing.com
For customer service and orders:
Toll-Free 1-888-313-2665

Visit us on the Internet at www.arcadiapublishing.com

Milton's riverfront today shows no trace of its once bustling activity. Warehouses and stores no longer line the water's edge with wharves stretching out into the river. No boats are anchored by the shipyard, awaiting repair. Lighters loaded with lumber no longer head downstream as the Tampa and Swan steam into Milton with their daily cargo and passengers. Now they lie on the bottom of the Blackwater. Only the river remains.

Contents

Acknowledgments		6
Introduction		7
1.	Downtown Milton	11
2.	Greater Milton	49
3.	Good Times, Bad Times	73
4.	Lumber Towns	87
5.	Other Towns	107

Acknowledgments

On behalf of the Santa Rosa Historical Society, I would like to express our great appreciation to those who shared their family photographs, for without their trust and assistance, this book would not have been possible; those special people are as follows: Millard Adams Sr.; Jennifer Byrom; Mary C. Findley (Diamond family); Jerry Fischer; Margaret Broxson Gillis (Harter family); Elizabeth Diden Gillman; Henry Gilmore; Lewis Golson Harrison; Ernestine Lynn Hobby; Bruce Johnson; Buddy Jordan (Oliver Jernigan Collection); Martha Walker Penfield; Anne Pinckard (Penton Collection); Joyce Penton Schnoor; Mary and Obie Willis (Brashears family); Kathryn Wilkinson; Mary Beth Williamson; Tom Serviss, at the Blackwater River State Forest; and Dean Debolt, Special Collections, University of West Florida.

We are also grateful to our members whose photographs form the basis of the society's collection, but who are no longer with us: Nell Byrom, Christine Thames Green, Rusty Grundin, Father James Gilligan, Mary Emma McDaniel Villar, Frank Penton, Merna Urquhart, and Wiley Williams Jr.

I would also like to thank Nathan Woolsey for his assistance and to thank both Dr. Brian Rucker and Nathan for writing the introduction. It is from these two young men that future chronicles of Santa Rosa County will come. A thank you should also go to all the society's members whose continued financial support make the preservation of our heritage possible.

Unfortunately, some towns are not represented in this book merely because we were not aware of any photos of them in existence. The Santa Rosa Historical Society hopes readers will help correct this by sharing their photograph collections with us.

Introduction

Hundreds of years ago, if one were sailing up the Blackwater River, a series of wooded bluffs would appear on the western bank. Located 2 miles north of the bay, the point of the river where the saltwater changes to freshwater was wide and deep, and a small creek also emptied into the river here. This was the future site of Milton.

Native Americans frequented the area and used the western bank of the river as a trail into the interior. And though the Spanish permanently settled Pensacola in the late 1690s, this region of Florida remained unsettled and undisturbed. Not until a British interval in the 1760s through the 1780s did a European presence take root—when a few intrepid individuals established a shipyard and homes in the vicinity of present-day Milton and Bagdad. After the British left, the area once more became deserted, save for occasional brave curious souls exploring the danger-filled interiors of Spanish Florida.

With the U.S. acquisition of Florida in 1821, numerous Americans from various Southern states moved into Florida, and pioneer settlements began to appear at the head of Blackwater Bay. The origins of Milton itself are relatively obscure. The town basically emerged from the "Blackwater Settlement" of the 1820s and 1830s, a community that stretched from the mouth of Clear Creek at Jackson Morton's brickyard down to Pelican Bayou on Blackwater Bay. As opportunistic Americans harvested the rich virgin forests of longleaf yellow pine, the site of Milton became the natural location for a river landing. Timbermen floated rafts of lumber from the forests upstream to the series of bluffs upon which a settlement gradually took root.

Benjamin and Margaret Jernigan were two of the first settlers in Milton in the 1830s, and they owned extensive acreage and constructed the settlement's first industry—a water-powered sawmill at present-day Locklin Lake. This early mill is probably the origin of Milton's name.

By the late 1830s, the community boasted a ferry crossing, a lumber landing, a voting precinct, and a general store. The site went by a number of colorful names before permanently being labeled "Milton." In the 1830s, it was referred to as "Black Water," "Lumberton," "Jernigan's Landing," "Hard Scrabble," and "Scratch Ankle." The name "Scratch Ankle" reputedly came from the many briars that grew along the river bluffs on which the settlement was built, so when people landed from the river, the briars would scratch their ankles.

By 1839, though, the town was being referred to as "Milltown," or "Milton," and the next year Milton obtained its own post office. In 1842, Santa Rosa County was created, and the centrally located town of Milton became the logical site for the county seat. Two years later, the rapidly growing town of Milton was officially incorporated.

Antebellum Milton was centered primarily along the waterfront bluff on Blackwater River, where Willing Street comprised the chief business district. Another key street was Berryhill, which led to the ferry landing on the river. The county's courthouse was erected on this thoroughfare, and the road extended westward to the Berry Hill, the high ground west of Milton Cemetery, and proceeded farther to Arcadia, Mulat, Floridatown, and points beyond.

Thanks to the plentiful pine forests, Milton grew vibrantly in the years before the Civil War. By the early 1850s, the town held some seven hundred inhabitants, and one citizen from 1851 wrote a splendid description of the city:

"The navigation [to Milton] is excellent for steamboats and sail vessels . . . and is the best location for business in West Florida. We have six large stores, which sell annually from $30,000 to $70,000, and in the vicinity of the town, one large cotton factory in full operation, two steam saw mills, running each 33 saws, one steam sash and door factory, two steam planing mills, one pail and bucket factory, a new steam mill progressing rapidly to a state of completion which will run a like number of saws, which when completed will make ninety-nine saws all running within sight of each other; we have three ship yards, and three confectioneries. . . .We have also one Blacksmith shop, one Bakery and two large and commodious Hotels. . . ."

By 1860, Milton was Florida's seventh largest city, with a population of 1,815. The county's sawmills (Santa Rosa was Florida's most industrialized county that year) accounted in part for Milton's growth. Milton's wharves were also lined with cotton from southern Alabama cotton growers, who would bring their crops south for transportation down Blackwater River. Farmers from the interior made the town a convenient market place. Milton had even applied for—but unsuccessfully—port of entry status, and rival Pensacola businessmen sometimes expressed economic concern over Milton's thriving enterprises. The town in 1860, on the eve of the Civil War, boasted a healthy business district of stores, sawmills, wharves, hotels, and shipyards. There was a Masonic Lodge, several churches and schools, and a newspaper.

Unfortunately, storm clouds descended upon the South the following year, and Milton, as well as other areas of West Florida, faced Union blockading forces at the mouth of Pensacola Bay that effectively stopped local commerce and coastal trading. Despite these threats, Frederick Howard's shipyard in Milton began construction of a 150-foot, wooden gunboat for the Confederate States Navy. The gunboat never saw service, however, for in the spring of 1862, when Confederate forces evacuated Pensacola, a controversial scorched-earth policy was implemented and the Milton gunboat, along with businesses and other resources, were torched by retreating Confederate soldiers.

West Florida became a no-man's land in the Civil War. Many Milton families abandoned the town and moved into the safety of southern Alabama towns like Greenville, Pollard, and Evergreen. Confederate pickets occasionally frequented Milton, always on the guard for Union expeditionary raids launched from the Pensacola area. On several occasions Federal troops raided Milton both overland and by steamboat, and small skirmishes took place in the streets between the opposing forces. Many homes and businesses were looted, and Milton took on the appearance of a ghost town. One Confederate soldier who visited Milton during the war saw only nine men and noted the town was "completely sacked as the old city of Troy."

By 1865, the Confederacy was crumbling both from within and without, and West Florida's citizens were facing increasing Union raids, a total economic collapse, roaming bands of outlaws, and other hardships. On April 9, 1865, Robert E. Lee surrendered his Southern forces in Virginia, essentially ending the conflict. And on April 25, 1865, Confederate forces from southern Alabama under General James Clanton surrendered to Union officers in Milton. The war was over.

Citizens returning to Milton in the summer of 1865 found the town broken and looted and its waterfront mills, foundry, and shipyard burned. Recovery looked to be a long, hard road, indeed. In 1867, the Freedmen's Bureau warden, Col. Henry Gansevoort, described Milton as "a place of no particular importance, situated in a lumber district, and buried in the pine woods," but it was that "lumber district" that soon brought new life to the town. Northern and

European capital was rebuilding local sawmills within months of Appomattox as returning Confederates laid down their arms and took up the woodman's axe. In the vicinity of Milton alone, Farrar Hughes & Co. opened on Quinn Bayou in 1866, and Greenberry Dycus reopened his mill on Magnolia Basin that same year. In 1868, George Marquis opened a third steam-powered sawmill on the basin over the Blackwater that still bears his name.

Despite a sharp downturn in the lumber market in 1867, the years of Reconstruction were fairly good economically, sparing Santa Rosa the turmoil and strife that marked Florida's cotton counties to the east. By 1870, conditions had become so rosy that the state legislature even chartered the "Santa Rosa Railroad, Banking, and Insurance Company" with a capital stock of $2 million "to be located in the town of Milton." Midwife to the plan was Milton's representative carpetbagger, John W. Butler of Massachusetts, a jovial, big-hearted rogue who once boasted that in Milton he held "thirteen offices . . . and growl[ed] like hell because I can't get another." Butler's arch-foe, lawyer George G. McWhorter, was another Milton resident and was the leader of Santa Rosa's Democrats, who became "Speaker in Assembly" of the Florida House at the end of Reconstruction in 1877. For services rendered the Republican Party, Butler received a federal posting to Salt Lake City in 1878 and never returned. In his stead, Santa Rosa Republicans were led for more than forty years by the quiet dignity of Alexander Jackson, a former slave and Milton native who had distinguished himself as a black Union soldier in the Civil War.

However, by the autumn of 1873, Milton's boom had gone bust. A Panic on Wall Street set off a national depression that effectively brought the town's prosperity to an end. The year and mood of 1874 more than recalled the dark days of 1862. Recovery was slow, and economic doldrums would persist until the coming of the railroad to Milton a decade later. Notwithstanding, a new two-story courthouse, utilizing brick from John Hunt's antebellum yard on Blackwater Bay, was completed by July 1877, featuring a fireproof vault, a slate roof, and a cupola for a town clock. Despite the novelty of Milton's first brick edifice, economic forces remained in hibernation. In 1878, the *Milton Standard* reported the following: "Interest in everything appears to have died out in Milton. An energetic man would be a curiosity. Sad." Clearly, what the town needed was a railroad connection to the outside world. Milton would live or die in its proximity to a Panhandle Line that would connect through to Tallahassee and beyond.

On June 1, 1881, construction began on the Pensacola & Atlantic Railroad, and on August 15, 1882, the first passenger train pulled into Milton. By 1885, Milton even had its own railroad turntable, so the "down train" could return to Pensacola "head first." Though many predicted the town's "prestige as a (logging) supply depot for a vast interior county would be lost," as money flowed out east and west, Milton merchants paid no attention. By July 1883, John Carlovitz had the town's second brick building under construction at a cost of $6,000 to house a bakery. John Hoodless opened a shingle mill adjacent to his shipyard. Joseph Amos contemplated the erection of a "mammoth hotel" for the winter tourist trade. Milton even gained recognition for its natural history museum—three hundred specimens of which were exhibited at the New Orleans World Exposition in 1884.

Then, in the midst of this early flowering, disaster struck. A fire in the store of Mayer Bros. spread out of control and burned down Milton's business district on May 20, 1885. A second fire on April 2, 1892, again burned out the entire business district, consuming the accrued wealth of seven years' prosperity, just as America was slipping toward its second great depression since the Civil War.

Nevertheless, in 1885, progress brought Milton the sawmill of James A. Chaffin & Co., which was constructed on the site of the McVoy mill, burned in the Civil War. Residents were less than thrilled with the prospect of smoke from the slab kiln drifting down over the town, but they greatly appreciated the firm's payroll. The year 1885 also brought Milton the steam-powered gristmill of Davison & Webb, erected near the depot and joined by an ice plant by 1896. By 1890, the shingle mill of Cater Bros. was in operation, while nine hundred shares of the Milton canning factory were fully subscribed. By the summer of 1891, canned fruits, vegetables, and fish under the Milton label were appearing in stores throughout the region. Much of this economic activity met doom in the four long years of depression that shackled America between 1893 and 1897. With little more than the Chaffin mill making it through to century's end, boom and bust had become a way of life for the town of Milton.

As Milton entered the twentieth century, the town, once known for its Yellow Fever, hard drink, and "justice" by noose and gun, was still a raucous, clapboard, two-fisted town of mud streets and corrugated iron. Within a few years, however, this backwater lumber burgh became a prosperous model city of the Progressive Age. Ironically, its coming affluence was partly set in motion by the forces of utter destruction, when a devastating fire on January 31, 1909, leveled the whole business district. Willing Street merchants had barely recovered by 1911 when an overturned kerosene lamp set off yet another conflagration that was only contained by the timely arrival of the Stearns and Culver fireboat from Bagdad. Willing Street businesses were rebuilt with brick, and by 1915, Milton boasted of a brick power plant, Opera House, Exchange Hotel, Canal Street School, and a bridge over the Blackwater. With the purchase of the first auto firetruck in all of west Florida, Milton would never again suffer a disastrous fire.

Concurrent with the structural improvements was an increasing cultural influence. Instrumental in civilizing the town was the "dry law" of 1907, thirteen years before national Prohibition. Three saloons on Willing Street were closed, and the sheriff was kept busy raiding moonshine stills—their illegal contents being poured into the rivers. The moving pictures at the Opera House were censored by the owner, with "none of an immoral or degrading character being permitted." The women of the town formed literary and civic organizations, including the Ladies Red Cross. Farmers, ranchers, and woodmen organized as did the Chamber of Commerce and Navy League. Girls had their Canning Club and boys had their Corn Club, which sponsored the yearly Corn Fair Day on courthouse square. Baseball teams were organized, along with a Milton band; however, attempts to start a Milton orchestra were unsuccessful. This sudden plethora of clubs was parodied by a group of men who formed the Overall Club, dedicated to the wearing of overalls.

The town reveled in its progress, despite the closing of three shipyards after the First World War. The construction boom continued into the twenties with a new courthouse, town hall, and Berryhill School. A new Blackwater Bridge and brick paving in 1921 and Escambia River Bridge in 1926 made Milton more accessible. Northern land speculators inundated the area, buying up huge tracts of land. Santa Rosa County was touted as the "Fruit Belt of the South," and thousands of satsuma orange trees were planted along with grapes, apples, peaches, etc. These ambitious plans came to an end with the Crash of 1929. Santa Rosa suffered a double blow because its savior in years past, the pine trees, were just about gone. The Depression brought hard times, but despite individual hardships, the county on the whole benefitted. Through government programs, Milton gained a new water and sewer system, school, and post office, while the county gained paved roads, rural electrification, schools, and the Blackwater River State Forest. Recovery was given an added impetus by the establishment of Whiting Field in 1942.

Although retaining its small-town atmosphere into the sixties, Milton is now seeing burgeoning growth. The early settlers of Santa Rosa County would be amazed at the transformation of their home.

Brian R. Rucker
Nathan Woolsey
Laurie Green

One
Downtown Milton

The brick road known as old Spanish Trail, or State Road 1, was built from Milton eastward toward the county line in 1919–1921. Originally only 6 miles long and 9 feet wide, concrete shoulders were added in 1926 to make it a two-lane road. Renamed U.S. Highway 90 in 1929, it was converted to local use when a new highway was put in parallel to it in 1955. It is one of the very few extant brick roads with sections still in use today.

Looking north from the railroad bridge, this view of the the waterfront shows some of the damage sustained after a 1916 storm. In the distance is the old Chaffin sawmill, which had already closed by 1903. The mill was reopened by C. Mayo in 1913 and a planing mill added in 1918. Known also as the McGowin Mill, and after 1921 the Lynn Mill, it survived fires, floods, and timber shortages until it closed permanently in 1937. H.C. Woods was the last owner.

In the early 1920s, the cross-tie business was second only to the mills, but it lasted just a few years. Rafts of up to three thousand ties, cut from logs left as unusable by the lumbermen, were floated downstream to be loaded onto lighters such as the *Valparaiso* and *Elmira*. Individuals were paid 14¢ per tie by local dealers, such as H.C. Woods and the Rollo Brothers.

For almost a hundred years, the only way to cross the Blackwater was a ferry that docked at the foot of Berryhill Street. This bridge opened in 1916, with a trestle extension across the swamp added in January 1917. In May, it was knocked off its foundation by the lumber lighter, *Dixie*, and was repaired only to be destroyed later by a hurricane in September 1917. This boat is the *Natomah*, a millionaire's yacht converted to commercial use. It made daily trips to Pensacola.

The three-car ferry was reinstated until a second bridge was completed in September 1921. Built by Pensacola Shipbuilding Co., it featured a bascule lift span instead of a turnstile. In 1923, when the county "repaved" it with sand and oil, the lift quit working until the extra weight was removed. The bridge keeper took a 24-hour vehicle count on the twenty-fourth of each month. By 1924, one thousand cars a day were crossing the bridge, many from out of state.

The 110-foot steamer *City of Tampa* made daily trips to Pensacola with stops at Bay Point and Bagdad for more than twenty-five years. It was owned by Captain William Barry (engineer) and Captain Charles Mason (navigator). Will Walker was the fireman. Capable of carrying 160 passengers, the steamer left Milton at 6:30 a.m. and arrived in Pensacola at 10:00 a.m., returning to Milton by 5:30 p.m. with fresh bread, snapper, and bananas for resale. The steamer caught fire in 1921 and floated downriver aflame until it sank off Bay Point. She was replaced by *Sister* under Captain Mayfield.

The *Helmar* carried mainly freight on its daily trips to Pensacola. Its landing was by the Fisher-Hamilton warehouse. In 1924, Captain Aymard replaced her with the larger *Swan*, which came to Milton twice a week. In 1926, she was replaced by the smaller *Grady S*, as more freight was traveling over the new Escambia River Bridge. A year later, the *Swan* burned in Marquis Bayou. Ships continued to make the Milton-Pensacola run into the thirties.

The Hoodless Shipyard, at the southern end of the waterfront, had been in operation since 1870. Having three marine ways, it specialized in repairs, occasionally launching schooners, smacks, and lighters. In 1917, Bagdad Shipbuilding Co. opened in the old planing mill next door, prompting Hoodless to install a new sign, "The Milton Shipyard." A third yard, Santa Rosa Marine, opened on the east riverbank a mile north. (Photograph courtesy of Special Collections, University of West Florida Library.)

In 1918, within six months, four ships were launched from the three yards. After the First World War, the shipyards closed, although Hoodless was leased briefly in the 1920s and built ten barges. Shipbuilding was revived for a few years in the 1930s, when Joe Scruggs ran a successful yard on Marquis Bayou, building small pleasure boats and Navy rescue boats for downed pilots. (Photograph courtesy of Special Collections, University of West Florida Library.)

Milton celebrated the completion of the bridge and brick road with a huge party for ten thousand people on Labor Day, 1921. It started with a parade that went to the end of the brick road and back, ending at Marquis Bayou, where a barbecue and fish fry feast had been prepared. A baseball game, swimming contest, and fatman's race kept folks entertained until nightfall when Caroline (then Grace) Street was closed off for a dance on the new brick paving.

When E.H. Lundy bought the Ollinger building in 1920, the old general store had already been turned into a garage. In 1925, he added a four-room addition that extended over the water. The upstairs was rented to realtor and the garage to Stewart. The downstairs was a ladies' restroom. Known as the Riverside Garage for many years, it was torn down in 1984. Lundy also had large land holdings in Allentown and later became a state senator.

George Creary ran the town's largest mercantile establishment here until 1903, after which the building became a saloon and pool room. The county went dry in 1907 and the building became Fisher-Hamilton Hardware. It is one of the oldest structures in the downtown area, probably dating from after the 1892 fire. In 1918, Hamilton sold his interest to C.M. Gainer and C.M. Andrews, and in 1922, Fisher sold his half to Sam Cox, but the store retained its well-known name until it closed in the sixties. This photo is from the early 1920s.

This unknown store sold farm equipment, wagons, and buggies as Fisher-Hamilton did. After a 1934 fire that burned the pool hall and coffin factory next door, Fisher-Hamilton advertised the following items in their fire sale: plows, axes, auto tires, roofing, screening, cookstoves, brooms, carpet sweepers, smoothing irons, and muzzles. In the fifties, their inventory included Haviland china and Fostoria crystal.

Milton's first courthouse was a wooden structure located on the present site of Berryhill School Center. It burned in 1869, destroying all records. Space was rented over the Ollinger store until a new red-brick courthouse was built in 1877 on the northeast corner of courthouse square, facing Willing Street. The bell up the ladder on the left was used as a fire alarm. Overcrowded and unsafe, the structure was torn down after the present courthouse was built in 1927.

Both the county judge and the town's justice of the peace had offices in the courthouse, seen in this 1913 or 1918 photo. The majority of cases were for "blind tigers" (whiskey purveyors), since Milton went dry in 1907. Two saloons across from the courthouse were closed down. There were occasional night-time shootings in the street, into the early twenties, and although the perpetrator was known, the verdict was usually self-defense because there were no witnesses to refute it.

This 1907 view of Willing Street, looking north, shows the courthouse with the cupola and the jail. The sheriff's family lived on the second floor, and the cells were in the back. They were often empty because prisoners were leased out to the mill owners until 1924. A porch was added on three sides in 1908–9. The last of the trees was cut down in 1921 to facilitate the new brick paving. The city also had a small jail around the corner on Caroline Street, and later along the waterfront.

The courthouse was the center of activity for any important meeting or celebration, such as this one originating here. The square was made into a park by the Ladies Civic League in 1917. They removed billboards, planted trees, and had a bandstand, benches, and swings installed. A new bandstand was donated by the Chamber of Commerce in 1946. Originally three small buildings, the telegraph, temporary town hall (the small-frame building was rented for only twelve years), and town jail were located on the north side facing Caroline Street.

The Board of County Commissioners posed in front of the old courthouse in 1913. Pictured from left to right are as follows: (front row) J. Baggett Jr., J. Hart, W. Barnes, H. Bowers, J. McArthur, J. Johnson, and W. Whitmire; (back row) J.T. Nowling of Jay, Peter Diamond, Sheriff Harvell, Oliver Jernigan Jr., and H.W. Thompson of Bagdad.

The old courthouse was already overcrowded by 1914 and then declared unsafe in 1922. Pensacola architect Chandler Yonge designed the present courthouse in "Classic Monumental" style. Hugger Construction Co. of Montgomery built it for $137,000 in six months. The building was dedicated on July 4, 1927. The jail was on the third floor but was removed in 1960 because of structural problems; additions were added at the same time, altering the four identical facades.

From the beginning, Milton had several active fraternal organizations. Organized in 1892, the Knights of Pythias built their hall (seen here) on Oak Street across from courthouse square. It burned in the 1909 conflagration that consumed much of Milton. The Pythians rented space until 1955, when they built a new castle home on Clara Street. The Masons (Santa Rosa No. 16 F & AM) were organized in 1846 and built their present hall in 1855. It was moved in 1915 to make room for the Canal Street School. (Photograph courtesy of Special Collections, University of West Florida Library.)

On a Sunday afternoon, May 3, 1914, the newly "hatched" members of the fraternal organization Nest of Owls #1662 posed for this picture in front of the old courthouse. The jail is in the background.

John Allen's meat market was located between the jail and Gainer's corner store (on left) on the southwest side of Willing Street from 1910 (about when this picture was taken) to 1925. It was torn down when the new courthouse was built. There was another butcher shop across from the courthouse that installed electric refrigeration in 1925.

Frequent trips to a meat market such as this one in 1912 were necessary because of a lack of refrigeration. Even in the forties, people depended on the daily delivery of an ice block for their ice box. Milton had an ice plant located across from the depot as early as 1896. The ice plant also stored meat, and after 1931, slaughtered and cured it. Individual, keyed lockers were installed in 1946 for private food storage.

J.C. Gainer had a grocery store on the corner of Willing and Oak Streets since 1892. He retired when the County bought the property for the new courthouse in 1926. His son continued the family business with a store and gas station across the street for several years.

In 1921, Urquhart's grocery store offered canned goods and bins of onions and potatoes, along with kerosene lamps, even though electricity had been available nearly ten years. From left to right, Frank Slater, Sam Grain Jr., J.W. Urquhart, Jack Driggers (child), Howard Tompkins, Mr. Jernigan, Buddy Stewart, and Sam Grain Sr. stood behind the counter where a roll of brown paper sat ready to "bag" purchases.

The northwest corner of Willing and Caroline Streets was occupied by Jernigan's grocery store until First National Bank built a substantial brick building on the site in 1908. The second floor was rented by attorneys, realtors, and insurance agents. First National was a mainstay of Milton's financial life until, through mergers, it became SunTrust Bank today. This building burned in the 1909 fire, but the bank's officers rented space until a new structure was built.

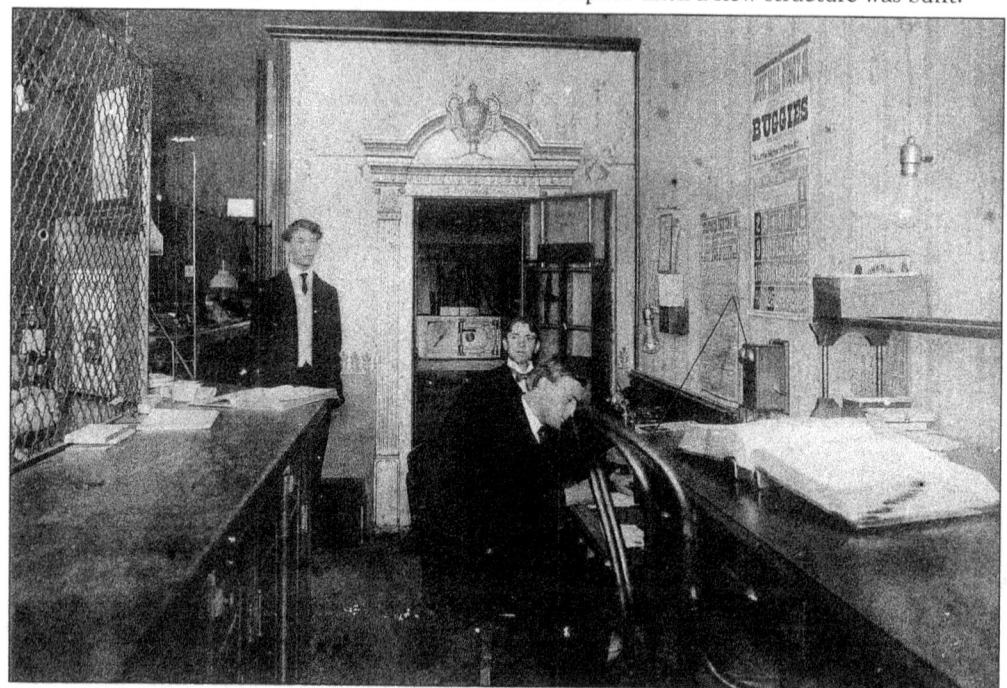

The Chaffin Bank opened in 1908 on the northeast side of Willing Street, and closed, in good standing, in 1917. It's location was taken over by Milton State Bank in 1920, but it too closed in 1932. It was never as large as First National. Arlie Mann is standing on the left in this 1908 photo.

The second First National Bank built in 1910–11 was even larger than the first. It included eight offices, a barbershop, and two storefronts, one of which was often used as a cafe. The town council rented space for $150 a year until 1916, when it rented a small building on Caroline Street behind the courthouse for $25 less and a second small building next to it for the city jail. This photo from the early twenties shows the yellow brick as it was originally; over the years a stone-brick facade was added.

First National caught fire on July 23, 1968. The clock stopped at 9:53 a.m. Volunteer firemen from Milton, East Milton, Bagdad, Pace, Skyline, Jay, and Whiting Field fought for five hours to get the inferno under control. Citizens and firemen formed lines to hand out bank records and files from the law offices upstairs. A short but heavy rain at one o'clock and again at two o'clock did little to diminish the fire, but did wet down the roofs of neighboring buildings, preventing a repeat of the 1909 fire.

The Milton Opera House, or Milton Auditorium, was designed by Walker Willis and built by S.F. Fulghum and Sons in 1913. The upstairs theater showed silent movies five times a week and had vaudeville shows on Saturday nights. A talking picture machine was installed in 1930. When the Gootch's bought the building in 1920, they renamed it after their eleven-year-old daughter, Imogene. It closed in 1946 and was used briefly as navy barracks. The Santa Rosa Historical Society bought the dilapidated building in 1984 and has restored it to its former glory. It looks better now than it did in this 1916 photo.

The first floor of the Opera House was divided between a storefront and the post office. Improvements to the latter, such as a wood floor and a metal net partition, were added in 1923 after this picture was taken. Patrons were requested to stop accosting the mailman as he left by the side door and to either wait for home delivery or rent one of the twenty-six new lock boxes. Today the worn granite threshold is the entrance to the Museum of Local History.

Before the historical society could begin restoration of the Imogene, forty years accumulation of rotted wood, wet plaster, partitions, and shower stalls had to be torn out. A new set of stairs and fire escapes provided access for the volunteers, while a new roof kept them dry. The wooden dance floor was removed, to be reused in the foyer. Then, before the major renovation could start, the reinforced concrete floor had to be load-tested. Eight king-sized waterbeds were used for the test, after which they were drained, moved, and refilled again, and again.

The interior of the restored Imogene Theatre shows the result of hundreds of hours of volunteer labor and $250,000 in state preservation grants. The large stage, wooden dance floor, and tiered balcony on three sides make it an ideal setting for the plays, recitals, and dances the historical society has sponsored. It is also rented out for weddings and parties. Because of the Imogene, people are once again coming to downtown Milton on Saturday nights.

Although at various times the Imogene had competition from a Ritz, a Rex, and a Palace Theater, it remained the staple entertainment not only for movies, but also dances and parties. Here servicemen from the new Whiting Field in 1943–5 line up for a show. It closed when a large, modern theater opened in 1946, although the stores on the ground floor continued to operate for twenty-five years.

A view of Caroline Street looking eastward toward the bridge shows the original brick paving where it meets the concrete pavement added around the courthouse in 1927. The streets were widened on all four sides to provide parking. Harrison and Estes had the lowest bid to pave the parking areas and sidewalks to each of the four doors. Glen St. Mary's nursery provided the landscaping. Almost all the city streets were paved by 1930.

R.J. Allen and his employees stood in front of his garage and taxi service around 1914–5. The building was leased to Mitchell and Lundy Garage in 1916 for a few years, after which it became Allen-Faircloth Motor Co., a Ford dealership. It was rebuilt after the 1917 hurricane caused the roof to cave in. A large addition was put on the back in 1930–1, closing off the alley. Known for many years as Rozier Ford and then Gentry Ford, the building later became a department store. It is presently the Breadbasket Restaurant and offices.

The Allen Garage was one of the earliest in Milton, having been built on the site of an old livery stable. Not until the late twenties did garages and service stations proliferate. In 1913, there were only six cars, but by 1930, 1,902 cars were registered and accidents, some fatal, were increasing. In 1923, the sheriff got a high-speed motorcycle to catch anyone going over 30 miles per hour (10 miles per hour in town). After 1926, children under fourteen could not drive without a parent present.

In 1895, Milton had three hotels, also used as boardinghouses for mill workers: the Commercial Hotel on Broad Street, the Johnston Hotel on southeast Willing, and the third which was enlarged and renamed the Waldorf Hotel by 1903. It was owned by Dr. C.O. Chunn, who had a dentist office on the second floor, and his wife, who had a millinery shop on the first. The Waldorf was located on the corner of Caroline and Elmira Streets; this is the side facing Elmira. The street in the foreground is Walnut, now part of the city parking lot.

Another view of the Waldorf, this time looking north on Elmira, shows a house on the present site of the Exchange Hotel. The main road westward, now Caroline Street, had to detour around this house and the Waldorf onto Walnut. Courthouse square would be on the right and the Johnson, Green, Miller & Gibson law firm is now on the corner once occupied by the Waldorf.

Milton had devastating fires in 1885 and 1892, but the one on January 31, 1909, was the worst. It started in Fisher's Dry Goods Store at 3:30 a.m. on a Sunday morning. Fanned by cold winds, it quickly spread to both sides of north Willing Street, then to First National, and then to the Waldorf, leaving only the chimneys seen above. The fire crossed the back of courthouse square, sparing the courthouse and south Willing Street, but burning the Knights of Pythias Hall on Oak Street.

By the time the fire was extinguished, twenty-two buildings had been destroyed, including three houses. Pensacola's steam fire engine had been called at 5 a.m. and put on a railroad car, arriving here at 9 o'clock. However, by that time, the people's bucket brigade had gotten the fire under control. Not much remained of north Willing Street or the brick bank on the left. Another fire in 1911 burned the buildings on south Willing.

These participants in the auto and horse parade, along with the Pensacola Band, opened the first county fair on November 4, 1910. It was staged under four large tents on the site of the Waldorf Hotel. Mr. Simpson of Arcadia had the best display of farm produce and livestock.

In 1923, R.J. Allen built the first all reinforced concrete building in Milton on the Waldorf site. It was planned as a fireproof hotel with twenty-four rooms with private baths, but the second floor was leased as offices before it ever opened. Allen opened the Rex Theater in the middle section of the building for a short time and a porch furniture factory in the corner section. For many years it was also the home of Powers-Martin and later Gillman Furniture and the *Press Gazette*. The Johnson-Green law firm remodeled it in 1971.

The Exchange Hotel was "copied" from the Milton Auditorium by Charles Sudmall, who admired the new theater. He hired the same contractor, S.F. Fulghum of Pensacola, to build a telephone exchange, but upon its completion in 1914, he moved the exchange to a frame structure next door and leased the building to H.L. Creary, who opened the Exchange Hotel. It changed hands several times, becoming a rooming house during World War II. The building fell into disrepair until 1983, when Bill Rosasco restored it. Sudmall had just sold the phone exchange in 1925, when he was killed by eight bullets—the ruling was self-defense.

Haywood Hanna was manager of both the Imogene and the Ritz Theater on south Willing when he built a deluxe 900-seat theater next to the Exchange Hotel. He moved the equipment from the Ritz and opened the new theater on August 14, 1946. Admission, popcorn, and a soft drink was 25¢. In 1950, Hanna also built the Joy Drive-In Theater on Highway 90 in East Milton. A second drive-in was located on the northern end of Stewart Street.

Mr. Amos built the "5¢ & 10¢ Store" on Caroline Street behind the Exchange Hotel in 1946. Highway 90 was straightened, opening this new section, in 1937. Prior to that, Caroline Street ended at the Exchange, necessitating a turn onto Elmira and another on Walnut. The Florida Cafe was a popular restaurant until it closed in the seventies.

This service station was located on the triangular lot where the city parking lot by the Exchange Hotel is today. The first station was built here around 1928 and was later converted to the Hotel Cafe. A larger one that included the Firestone store, bus station, and a cafe was built in 1940. Ullys Hicks stands on the right.

The federal government announced in January 1939 that a new post office would be built "two blocks from town." The old Ellis-Williams House was moved from the site, and construction began in February 1940. A basement was built in the post office to house federal offices.

The post office was completed early in October, but the formal dedication was held on Armistice Day, November 11, 1940. Miss Kate McDaniel was postmistress. A large mural was painted through the auspices of the federal Public Works Administration. When the current post office was built, a 10-foot section of the mural was donated to the historical society and is displayed in their Museum of Local History.

Milton's first post office was, in 1885, the only building on the northwest end of Willing Street. The postmaster, John Carlovitz, lived in a house just north of the brick building, and he had a stationery shop in the front. (He also had a museum of natural history.) The structure survived the 1892 and 1909 fires, but the post office was moved to larger quarters in the Imogene in 1913. This building was used as a barbershop, store, and then a men's reading room in 1922. It was torn down in 1952.

The weekly newspaper the *Clarion* was published in 1898 by H.S. and A.R. Seabrook. By 1900, its name was changed to the *Milton Index*, and this office was opened on Willing Street, slightly north of First National. By 1910, the *Index* had been replaced by the *Milton Gazette*, with A.R. Seabrook as manager and George Childerson as editor.

In 1895, the northern side of Willing Street was still sparsely occupied. Howard Jernigan ran a drugstore on the corner, next to a general merchandise store owned by the McDavid brothers. The third store was Adams's jewelry store. Farther down the street, the Cohen brothers had a department store. In the distance is Dr. McDougall's Palace Drug Store and just out of sight is D.T. Williams's store. (Photograph courtesy of Special Collections, University of West Florida Library.)

Mr. Amos and friends posed for this photograph on Willing Street around 1900. Ernest Amos was an attorney who rented office space in the D.T. Williams Building. He was Florida's comptroller from 1917 to 1932. It was his old homesite that was purchased for the Milton High School on Stewart Street. (Photograph courtesy of Special Collections, University of West Florida Library.)

A cow meandered down Willing Street in 1914. Milton passed a "cow law" in 1916 that required owners to keep cows and pigs in their own yards. It was not strictly enforced, so most houses had fences and cow grates to keep out their neighbors' cattle. A limit of three cows per house was set. However, as late as 1941, free, roaming livestock was still a problem. The City had to double the fees for reclaiming impounded cows and hogs to $1 a head.

The same scene approximately ten years later shows the brick paving done in 1921. The hand pump and horse watering trough seen in the foreground was sold for scrap when the new courthouse was built in 1927. Note the 30-inch-tall post behind the car on the right. This red and white "traffic director" was imprinted with "Go Slow" in vertical lettering. Placed in the middle of the intersection in 1919, it was used until 1938, when Milton installed its first traffic light here. A second was soon put at Canal Street and Highway 90 for the safety of schoolchildren. Not until 1949 were lights added on Stewart Street and Munson Highway.

Willing Street in the early fifties was the business and shopping center of Milton. Besides Milton Drug Store with Dr. Thames's office above, there were also Weavers Drugs with Dr. Holley's office in the back and the Florida Pharmacy. Gulf Power and the gas company offices were on the right. In addition to the bank and Fisher-Hamilton Hardware, there were also two department stores, Cohens and Olen; a "dimestore"; jewelry and clothing stores; barbers; beauty

shops; cleaners; shoe repair shops; cafes; and professional offices. Stewart Street did not develop until it was extended from Berryhill south to U.S. Highway 90 near Spencer's Sawmill in 1946. At the same time, the Munson Road was also extended to intersect with Stewart Street, which was lined with huge oak trees until it was four-laned in 1975.

James Hampton Stewart and Dr. A.C. Carter stood in front of Milton Drug Store for this photograph around 1917. The building itself dates from after the 1909 fire, although there was already a drugstore on this corner in the 1880s. The old "customs house" can be seen on the right. Already a shoe repair shop by 1895, it has been reconstructed inside the historical society's museum.

Dr. Rufus Thames; his wife, Ora; and her brother, Clint Byrom, purchased the Stewart drugstore in 1920. Dr. Thames and his brother, Dr. Jim Thames, used the second floor for their offices. Clint Byrom, Joe Creary, Buddie Pace, and Dick Weaver (from left to right) stand by the soda fountain around 1925–30. It, too, is in the society's museum. The corner drugstore was a Milton landmark until it burned in 1986. It has since been restored and is now used for offices.

The *Milton Gazette* was located in the Gainer building south of the courthouse in 1910. It had moved to a spot very near the old Milton Index Office north of First National by 1917. Publisher D.R. Read (left) and editor Ed Straughn stood in front of their offices in 1921.

The interior of a newspaper office around 1903 shows the time-consuming job of typesetting by hand. The *Milton Press-Gazette* donated this equipment to the historical society, and it can be seen in its museum today.

Looking south on Willing Street from Berryhill around 1914, this view shows the Williams brothers' stores on the left. In 1937, they were converted into the Rex and then the Ritz Theater. Each store owner was responsible for building a boardwalk in front of his building. Bates Department Store built a concrete sidewalk that even crossed the unpaved street.

Saturdays were the busiest days in downtown Milton because the farmers came to town to buy their week's groceries and supplies, to catch up on the latest political gossip at the courthouse, and perhaps to see a show at the Auditorium or Imogene. The kids called it "Tight Shoe Day." Saturday store hours were 6 a.m. to midnight and 6 a.m. to 7 p.m. on weekdays in 1920, except for Thursdays, when they closed at noon. A sale such as this one at Fisher's Dry Goods was always popular, even in 1910–15.

Company K men waited to hike to Allentown in the summer of 1917. Organized in 1913 and mustered in as a hospital corps of the Florida National Guard on August 5, 1917, they were sent to Camp Wheeler in Macon, Georgia. Two thousand people turned out to see them off as they marched from the armory at the north end of Willing to the depot, led by the Milton Band. Most of them returned in January 1919. Their company flag hangs in the entrance to the courthouse. Memorial trees were planted at the Berryhill Ballpark for the nineteen men (sixteen white, three black) killed in the war.

D.T. Williams came from Coon Hill, near Chumuckla, around 1880 and was well established in the grocery business by 1885. He ran the largest and oldest grocery until he died at age 72 in 1937. His brother, Wiley Williams, ran another store next door.

An African-American parade marched north on Willing Street sometime between 1911 and 1921. Many blacks were employed by the mills, and some owned their own shops. Martin Patterson had a restaurant and later a large grocery store on Oak Street. He also acted as undertaker, for he owned a hearse and two matched black horses. Willie Mims had a blacksmith shop on Broad Street, and one woman ran a boardinghouse on Canal.

Krentzman's Department Store is on the right in this 1930s photo, looking south on Willing Street. It started as Bates-Krentzman in 1908, but H.S. Bates started his own store in 1919. Bates's store closed in 1930 and Ben Finklestein's Surprise Store closed in 1933, but Krentzman's remained open until 1950. The Cohen's Department Store was the longest lived, having been started in 1896 and was managed by four generations of Cohens before it closed in the sixties.

The Chaffin mill can be seen behind the commissary in this early-1900s photo. Known as the Grab All Store, it was located at the water's edge at the foot of Berryhill Street. It had its own wharf. Badly flooded in 1906 and 1917, the building was torn down by 1923.

The Phinley Smith Company store was located in the Ollinger building along the waterfront by the bridge. Irene Camel, behind the counter, and Langham Stokes were the owners. It became Lundy's Garage in 1920.

Milton's first official town hall was built by C.E. Emmett in 1928. The rented frame building the town had been using was torn down to make way for the new courthouse in 1927. Made of concrete and stucco, it was located on the triangle formed by Berryhill, Broad, and Willing Streets. It housed the volunteer fire department in the rear. The first auto firetruck in West Florida cost almost as much in 1915 ($4,500) as the building did ($4,811). It was torn down when the second city hall was built in 1961–2.

The town waterworks and electrical plant were built in 1913–4, although the town had some electricity supplied by Bagdad Land and Lumber for several years prior to this. It featured a wood-burning steam generator, a 100,000-gallon cement reservoir, and steel tank on a 100-foot tower. It operated only twelve hours a day, 6 p.m. to 6 a.m., until 1920. Gulf Power bought the power plant in 1928, the same year the City updated the water and sewer system. The building was torn down in the sixties, but the concrete tower bases are still part of the fire department park on Berryhill Street.

Two
Greater Milton

The entire enrollment of Santa Rosa Academy posed with their teacher, Mr. Stephens, around 1890 or 1895. The school was said to be located north of Collins Mill Creek, west of Stewart Street. The academic year lasted four months. The "little red schoolhouse," as it was also called, burned down in April 1900, when a commemorative poem to it was mentioned in the *Milton Index*.

The second Santa Rosa Academy was built on the old courthouse site, the present Berryhill School Center, around 1900. Each of the teachers, including the principal, probably taught two grades. It burned at ten in the evening on December 22, 1914, after a musical recital. Only the piano could be saved. Space was rented in the Masonic Hall until the brick Canal Street School was built in 1915, and then the Academy site became a ballpark.

The end of the school year party on May 12, 1914, featured a maypole on the lawn in front of the school. The Merchant home can be seen on the far right, and in the distance is a house that was built by D.T. Williams around 1913.

The boys' basketball team practiced on the dirt court in the Berryhill schoolyard in 1912. A girls' basketball team was organized in 1921. A regulation clay basketball court was built by the Masonic Hall in 1931, although there was also one by the Canal Street School.

Architect S.J. Welch designed Berryhill, Bagdad, and Holley Schools in 1925, when the Canal Street School became overcrowded. It was built by Charles Emmett for $27,000, and had eight classrooms, running water, indoor toilets, and steam heat. Six more classrooms, along with a cafeteria, were added in 1934 by the Civil Works Administration (CWA) and the Federal Employment Recovery Act (FERA). It held five hundred students in the first six grades.

The oldest part of this house is the two-story gabled section that dates from around 1857, when Attorney George McWhorter and his wife moved into their new home. They added a one-story wing on the left in 1876. When he died in 1891, after being the school superintendent, house speaker, and chief justice of Florida's Supreme Court, his family added a room on the right and replaced the wing with a two-story addition. The house was sold in 1924 to mill owner William Lynn and is still owned by his heirs today. The photo is from 1904.

This folk Victorian house on Berryhill was built in 1889 by Captain Rufus Milligan, a partner in the Milton Mill with Chaffin. It likely replaced an earlier Milligan residence, as the family had lived here since 1872. The house changed hands several times; Dr. Thames bought it for a hospital and then sheriff Henry Clay Mitchell bought it in 1927 to convert into apartments. An addition was added on the back in the late thirties while the Armistead-Whitmire family owned the gingerbread-trimmed house.

It is not known who built this house in the late 1800s, but Mrs. Ida McDaniel bought it from J.A. Bryant sometime after her husband died in 1916. She lived here with her four daughters, Kate McDaniel, Mary Emma Villar, Matt Monroe, and Annie Stewart, until it burned in 1956. It was on the corner of Canal and Berryhill, facing Canal. This photo was taken on March 18, 1954, after the second snowfall in fifty-five years.

Originally from Burnt Corn, Alabama, Dr. Jim and Dr. Rufus Thames put each other through medical college, and then came to West Florida to be mill doctors. Dr. Rufus started his private practice first and married Ora Byrom. They built the house at 104 Canal Street in 1914. Added onto in the 1920s, the original bungalow architecture was altered somewhat. Ora was one of the founders of the Shakespeare Club and Milton Library. Dr. Rufus Thames was chosen as "Florida's Outstanding Physician of the Year" in 1948.

A cow wandered on north Alabama Street in the early 1900s. Judge L.M. Rhoda's house on the right was near the northeast corner of the intersection with Munson Highway. Alabama Street was also known as the Brewton Road since it was the main road north; it went to the top of "Rhoda's Hill" and veered left, just as it does today. The tracks in the left foreground lead to a spring near where Manning's Grocery is now located. They built their present store in 1941, although they had a store there prior to that time.

A closer view of the spring on Rhoda's Hill shows the dearth of trees, most of which were cut down by the mills in the 1800s. The oldest house in Milton, the Giles house, was located on Alabama Street. The area was even referred to as Giletown. It was estimated to be between eighty and one hundred years old when it burned in 1922.

Judge L.M. Rhoda came to Bagdad as an eighteen-year-old immigrant in 1873. He married Anna Hankins, and they lived in this house from 1875 till his death in 1925. He was the justice of the peace for many years in addition to being manager of Marston and Finch Furniture store, mayor, city clerk, tax assessor, treasurer, councilman, and Grand Chief Templar of Florida. He published a monthly newspaper, *The Good Templar*, in the late 1800s. This house style was very popular in Milton, but few examples remain.

Leo, Alice, Laurie, Maggie, and Winnie Harter (from left to right) stood in front of their house at 502 Alabama Street in 1913. Bill Barnes's grocery store is in the foreground; his brother had another store across the street. Alabama Street had several stores and gas stations, whereas Stewart Street remained residential into the fifties. The house was torn down in the early forties when the current Broxson home was built.

The first Methodist church was on Conecuh Street, just off Berryhill, where the parsonage is today. The land was donated by Joseph Keyser and H.W. Thompson. Built after the Civil War, it burned in 1904, when a careless smoker started a fire in a neighboring house, burning both to the ground, along with a third building.

The second church was built in the same location in 1905–6. It, too, burned when sparks from the heat stove caught the roof on fire on Sunday, December 22, 1932. Only the grand piano and the pulpit were saved by rescuers who knocked a large hole in the wall. The congregation had already started a new building on Berryhill and had the basement completed, but a lack of funds during the Depression prevented completion until 1936. In the interim, parishioners met in the courthouse.

Riding or walking south on Conecuh Street in 1907, one had to go through the creek, which delighted the children but not their parents. It was the same on Alabama and Stewart Streets until a bridge was installed on Conecuh in 1923.

Milton's only "steamboat house" takes its name from the bow veranda that wraps around the front, much like the deck of a paddle-wheel riverboat. It was built by Wiley Williams Sr. in 1887. R.E. Peterson was the contractor. When the roof burned in 1928, the house was redesigned in the bungalow style. It has been restored by the McCalls and Hartsells.

In 1888, Wesley Allen, owner of a livery stable, moved into this residence, formerly the home of David and Isaac Mayer. (They had moved to Pensacola after their business was destroyed in the 1885 fire.) Allen's daughter, Minnie, married Spencer Collins in 1903, and in 1923, they moved this house south on Elmira Street to free the old lot for their new brick bungalow. This house is still located on Elmira but with the second story and porch removed.

The D.C. Diden home was built between 1900 and 1905 facing toward the Presbyterian church. The Didens had a grocery store, Diden's Cash House, in the Ollinger building and later at the foot of Berryhill. Mrs. Diden was a charter member of the Shakespeare Club. The house was sold for $300 in 1959 and torn down. The lumber was used to build three houses in Marianna. Directly across from the church was the Central Hotel in the early 1900s.

In 1866, Reverend J. Lewis moved from Alabama and began preaching Presbyterian services in the Methodist and Baptist churches. Two years later, he went to New Orleans and Mobile to solicit funds for a church building, returning with $645. Work began in March 1868 and was finished by that August. The congregation consisted of twenty-eight charter members. The building was bricked up and wings were added on each side for Sunday school classes in 1927.

On June 30, 1927, Judge Thomas F. West's Bible class met in the old church for the last time, before renovation began. Thomas West was the state attorney general from 1912 to 1917, after which he served on the state supreme court, becoming chief justice. West retired in 1925 and returned to Milton as a circuit judge. Judge West is third from the left on the second row. The preacher, Mr. Young, is fourth from the left on the back row.

In 1895, the First Baptist Church was located on the corner of Oak Street and Santa Rosa, facing the latter, the present site of the Episcopal parish house. It was moved to the corner of Canal and State Road 1 (Highway 90) and then sold in 1912. The Baptists rented the Masonic Hall until their new church was finished on the same site. (Photograph courtesy of Special Collections, University of West Florida Library.)

The second Baptist church was built on the corner of Canal and Caroline Streets, facing Canal. While it was being built in 1913, lightning damaged the cupola. In 1938, the church was turned to face the newly realigned Highway 90, and it was also raised and a basement was added. After the present church was built, the building was used as a funeral home. It was torn down in 1971.

Mount Pilgrim Baptist Church, established in 1866, was originally located on Canal Street. (Prior to that time, some of the congregation attended First Baptist.) The congregation purchased land for a larger church in 1911, and architect W.A. Rayfield of Birmingham had designed a new building when on the night of March 30–1, 1916, the church burned. The new brick sanctuary was completed on October 30, 1916. The bell and tower were added in the 1920s.

The old Ellis home was built in the late 1800s on the road that was to become Highway 90. Its location was selected as the site for the "new" post office, and the house was moved to the back of the lot. The Ellis's children were John B. Ellis, Mrs. Lizzie Monroe, and Mrs. Wiley Williams Jr., who owned the house when it was moved.

The "Santa Rosa Graded School" was designed by Walker Willis and built by S.F. Fulghum, the same duo responsible for the Imogene Theatre. The Renaissance Revival–style building opened in November 1915, but was soon outgrown. Space for the primary grades was rented in the nearby Masonic Hall, which had been moved from the school site. In 1922, a two-year normal school was added with three teachers and fifty-five students. The higher the grade one received on the certification exam, the higher the grade level one could teach.

It was not unusual for one teacher to have forty-five students, although the class size decreased dramatically as the grade level increased. Graduating seniors numbered eight to twelve. By the forties, that number had only increased to forty. In 1957, Milton graduated fifty-nine students; T.R. Jackson, nineteen; Jay, fifty-four; Munson, thirteen; Allentown, twelve; and Chumuckla, nine.

The Milton High basketball team of 1929 consisted of, from left to right, Broward Tompkins, "Dub" Rivenbark, unknown, Rusty Grundin, Coy Sanders, Monroe Jernigan, and Sanders Duke. Games were played outdoors on a court by the school until a gymnasium was built in East Milton in 1939.

The football team in the early forties had Rufus Thames, the younger, as quarterback. Starting out as the "Swamp Angels" in 1921, the name was changed to the "Wildcats" the following year. Their school colors were black and orange. They played on Overman Field in East Milton by the Magnolia Basin Road. In 1933, the baseball team built a 9-foot wooden fence around the field so that spectators would have to pay 10¢ admission to support the team. The field was lighted in 1940 by the Junior Chamber of Commerce.

The Women's Clubhouse on Oak Street was a joint project of the Shakespeare Club, founded in 1911, and the Women's Club, founded in 1916. They had purchased the lot in 1930, but due to the Depression, they were unable to build the house until 1938, and then only with the help of the City and Work Projects Administration (WPA). The room on the right front was the lending library started by the Shakespeare Club. The building was used as a USO during World War II, and then as the Milton Library until 1976, when it reverted to its original use as a women's clubhouse.

James Chaffin bought this house on Oak from Sheriff Isaiah Cobb in 1856 for $1,150. Chaffin owned a successful general merchandise store, but left the area during the Civil War, when he served in the Confederate Navy. He invested in the lumber market with partner Rufus Milligan during the Depression of 1873–78 and eventually owned three sawmills. In 1885, he rebuilt the Milton Mill, which had been burned by the retreating Confederates. This Greek Revival house is now the Clay, Fitzgerald and Brooks law office.

Dr. Charles McDougall, local physician and owner of the Palace Drug Store, bought this Gulf Coast cottage-style house in 1872 for his growing family. He became rector of St. Mary's Episcopal Church in 1887. After his death in 1916, his daughter continued to live in the house, and upon her death in 1951, she willed it to the church. It was the Episcopal rectory for many years and now serves as church offices.

The Episcopal congregation was organized in 1867 and bought property for a church building in 1875. Completed three years later, this Carpenter Gothic church still has two of the original stained-glass windows. The carved cypress interior woodwork was, according to tradition, done by shipwrights. The brass kerosene lamps, now electrified, were purchased by the Ladies Aid Society in 1877. The reconstructed bell tower in the back holds the original bell.

Joseph Ollinger was one of three brothers in partnership with Martin Bruce, who owned a very successful shipyard in Bagdad. Burned by the retreating Confederates, the shipyard was rebuilt after the war. By 1871, Joseph Ollinger left the firm to open a grocery and dry goods store in Milton, adding a saloon by 1885. His house on Pine Street was constructed by 1875, but was sold in 1896, when he retired to Atlanta. Owned by F.H. Cobb for sixty years, the home has been restored by George and Shirley Tilghman.

John W. Butler, the first Republican sheriff and legislator during Reconstruction, built this residence on Pine Street in 1870. The house changed hands several times, with H.L. Creary owning it in the early 1900s. The porch was modified and a large wing replaced with the present one during Brooks Thornton's ownership in 1912–1917. This photograph was probably taken soon after the changes were made. Captain and Mrs. Art Potter have restored the house and garden.

Oliver Jernigan Jr., a farmer, county commissioner, and president of the Chaffin Bank, lived at 303 Pine Street after his house on Munson Highway burned. He later sold the property to E.C. Elder, president of the State Bank. When Elder died, his wife, Zena Elder, rented out rooms. It burned in 1979.

Mr. Allison had a small store on this corner near the depot. The Brashears siblings, Laura, Lizzie, and James, bought the site and had the back of this house moved to the Henry Street location. They lived in the back portion while the front section was built. James died in an accident at the Bagdad mill in 1935.

The Pensacola & Atlantic Railroad was completed through west Florida in 1882. The first depot was built within a year, but it burned in 1907. There were daily trains to Pensacola, leaving Milton early in the morning and returning each evening.

The second depot was built in 1909. Electric lights were added in 1916 and indoor plumbing added in 1917, but the sole heating source remained a pot-bellied stove that is still used today. The depot was moved 6 feet back from the tracks in 1917 to make room for a "butterfly shed," a covered cement walkway for passengers. When it was repainted in 1922, the newspaper editor approved of the change from the traditional drab colors to the new bright ones, but did not mention what they were. The original colors of gray and olive green were used in the restoration.

Depot workers stood inside the baggage room of the depot in the early forties. Elijah Beasley, on the right, was station agent for fifty years. His successor was Jabez Waters. Passenger trains were discontinued, and the depot closed in 1973.

The depot was in great disrepair when the Santa Rosa Historical Society was formed in 1974 to save it. With the help of a small Bicentennial grant, the fledgling society was able to make basic repairs to the roof and repaint the unique building. It opened to the public on July 4, 1976, with the first Depot Day Festival. Since then, extensive restoration has been done by the society. It is now leased to the West Florida Railroad Museum and serves as the center of the annual Depot Days Folkart Festival held every November.

Skinny-dippers cooled off in Collins Mill Pond, now known as Locklin Lake, near Park Avenue. The pond was formed by damming up the creek to power a nineteenth-century gristmill, which can be seen in the background. William Davison also had a steam-powered gristmill built across from the depot in the 1880s.

S.G. Collins bought the Davison and Webb mill around 1901, and by 1910, this one had already closed and fallen into disrepair. The steam mill burned, along with the neighboring grocery and ice plant, in 1931 under suspicious circumstances that resulted in two murders. Bookkeeper Aubrey Gainer, acquitted of arson, was shot and killed, and then Collins himself was shot to death. No one was ever tried for the murders. (Photograph courtesy of Special Collections, University of West Florida.)

Whiting Field was started as an auxiliary field on April 12, 1943. The Byrne Organization of Alabama was hired to build the runways and basic buildings in ninety days. Using 4,500 workers, the organization finished construction in eighty days. Unknown to local townsfolk, 225 German prisoners of war from Fort Rucker were also used to clear the land. Whiting Field was commissioned on July 15, 1943.

A.J. Honeycutt was hired to build three hundred family dwellings in forty-five buildings, in addition to single men's quarters, a clubhouse, commissary, and cafeteria. By the time Whiting Field became a full naval air station in 1946, it had pavement equivalent to 197 miles of a two-lane road.

The Overpass Club, later the Overpass Cafe and Grocery, was opened by L.D. Lewis and Ausborne Johnson in May 1937, coinciding with the new concrete viaduct and fill that rerouted the east end of the Blackwater Bridge. Located on the north side of State Road 1 (Highway 90), past Ward Basin Road, the club was a popular gathering spot for lunches, dinners, and dances. Originally open twenty-four hours a day, the new owner J. Smith cut the hours to eighteen in 1944. It was also a grocery store and gas station.

Coming into Milton from the west, around 1930, one would see that State Road 1 (Highway 90) on the left was paved. The graded sand clay road to Bagdad is on the right. The present-day Lutheran Church would be in between. The Poor Farm was on the right where the county auditorium is today. Started in 1890, the farm was converted to a prisoner road camp by the forties.

Three
Good Times, Bad Times

On Wednesday night, September 26–7, 1906, Milton was hit by the worst hurricane in 170 years. By three o'clock in the morning, the wind velocity had reached 100 mph and Willing Street was inundated. The river was jammed for a half mile with floating lumber, lighters, and debris. Bagdad and Bay Point Mills were also badly damaged. Looking north, one can see the Chaffin Mill in the distance.

This photo was probably taken from the back of D.T. Williams's store, looking north at the commissary. The waters reached all the way to Broad Street. The men are trying to save a dog in the water.

Lower Willing Street was also badly flooded in the 1906 storm. While the buildings withstood the water, most store owners lost all their stock. The water ran over the countertops in the Ollinger building.

The floodwaters reached the depot, across the tracks from these boaters. The railroad bridge is in the distance; the ice plant is on the left. The Escambia River trestle was badly damaged, so the railroad chartered the *City of Tampa* to bring train passengers around the washed out portions of track for the two weeks needed for repairs.

"Old Cabbage Top" was the nickname given to this engine stranded near the livestock pens and ice plant across the street from the depot, where this picture was taken. Cattle were routinely shipped to larger markets from here. Another train made it to the Escambia River trestle before the water put out the fire in the firebox and left the train on its side with sixty loads of freight.

Bad storms also hit in July and October of 1916, but the September 28–29, 1917 hurricane had more disastrous consequences. The new bridge, only twenty months old, was hit by a lumber barge that had broken loose from its mooring by the mill. The barge became lodged under one of the bridge spans, tipping it slightly.

While people tried to decide what to do about the bridge and the barge, the rising river forced the bridge off its foundation. The bridge rode downriver atop the mass of logs all the way to the Bagdad Mill. In 1918, it was salvaged by the federal snag boat *Escambia* and reused over Clear Creek on the Milton-Allentown road in 1921.

A barge and cut lumber also jammed up against the railroad bridge. It was able to be saved, although the trestle east of the bridge was badly damaged.

As the 125 mph winds died down and the water receded, men worked to clear up the lumber jam near Marquis Bayou. Besides losing its cut lumber, the Milton Mill also lost some of its buildings and sixty percent of trees in the woods. It closed for thirty days to rebuild. Although some of the fallen trees could be salvaged, the turpentine industry was severely hampered.

The September 21, 1926 hurricane was not as strong as previous ones, but it lasted longer—thirty-six hours. The storm swept away both piers at Floridatown, knocking one pavilion off its foundation and demolishing the Satsuma Beach pavilion. The new Escambia River Fill was washed out, and the railroad was put out of commission for a month. The river rose 9 feet, mainly due to a high tide. The brick road by Marquis Bayou in east Milton is representative of some of the damage to roads and wires in Milton.

On March 15, 1929, Milton suffered massive flooding from two days of heavy rainfall. The Blackwater Bridge, looking eastward, was nearly covered. Holes had to be cut in the pavement to relieve the pressure. In the background is the Johnson House, later known as the McElrod house, and the Johnson pavilion. Johnson was the bridgetender.

M.E. Lambeth opened his grocery store on the southwest corner of Willing and Oak Streets in 1928. He moved to Pensacola in 1930, and Gainer's son operated a service station and grocery here. The building is from 1900, but a foundry was on this corner in the years after the Civil War.

Lower Willing Street was badly flooded again in 1929. The railroad bridge can be seen in the distance. Milton was luckier than Milligan, which only had three houses left standing. Pilots from the Pensacola Naval Yard flew relief missions to south Alabama towns that were inundated.

The Fourth of July was really celebrated in 1915, as five thousand people came by boat, train, ferry, and horseback. The parade of autos, mounted men, Boy Scouts, and brass band left the depot at 8:30 a.m. The procession was a half mile long and arrived on Willing at nine.

The parade was interrupted by the arrival of a hydroplane that flew here from the Pensacola Naval Yard in twenty-four minutes, or a mile a minute, at 4,000 feet. Captain Ballinger landed the "air-ship" on the Blackwater north of the railroad bridge after maneuvering for thirty minutes. The parade then proceeded to the racetrack, where the celebration continued.

In addition to the parade, there were many contests: pie-eating, shoe-mixing, best cake, greased pole, and races—foot, horse, scrub horse, and fatman. The married men won a tug-of-war with the single men. Speeches were followed by a ball at the Opera House.

The highlight of the festive day—Labor Day and any other celebration up into the fifties—was "The Tournament." Horseriders competed to capture three, 2-inch-diameter rings hanging from posts spaced 50 yards apart on a 9-foot-long lance as they rode by on their horses. Each rider had three tries. The saddle that Rusty Grundin won, along with his lance, is on display in the Museum of Local History.

In 1916, the newly formed Mardi Gras Association planned a huge three-day celebration that was repeated in 1917, but never again. It drew ten thousand people, and a special train was put on for Friday's "Pensacola Day." Governor Park Trammel was greeted at the depot and escorted to the local school, where he addressed the crowd.

The winning car in the auto parade was that of Mrs. D.R. Read, the only woman driver. With her in the car was, from left to right, Mrs. D.C. Diden (back seat, large hat), little Margaret Read (back seat, middle), Miss Carrie Dye (back seat, far side), and Mrs. L.C. Fisher (passenger seat). The car was decorated in green and white, and the ladies wore outfits to match. They won a silver loving cup.

This horse-drawn float had pennants proclaiming "Votes for Women." Even though women got the right to vote in 1920, only twelve out of the two hundred eligible women voted in the 1922 election. In addition to the parades, there was a Ferris Wheel, merry-go-round, and wild animal acts brought in by the Greater Sheesley Shows. Its tents took up two city blocks.

Queen Vashti Keen and King R.A. McGeachy appeared in front of the courthouse on a platform that was later moved behind the building and converted to a bandstand. They were chosen by ballots cast by the public during the previous two weeks. There was a coronation ball one night and a masked ball the next at the Opera House. Mayor John Collins is on the right.

Some members of the Harter family model the latest swimwear for this photograph.

The Boy Scouts built this dam on Pond Creek to create a reservoir from which Bagdad Land and Lumber Company drew its water. After finishing, the boys went for a swim in 1927–8.

The Boy Scouts went on a camping trip to Turkey Bluff, on the west side of Pond Creek near the Highway 90 bridge. It was made into a park in 1913, redone by the American Legion in 1938, and the State in 1947. As late as 1955, the Scouts would go camping on Berryhill just past the cemetery, in the still-undeveloped woods.

A baseball team was organized in July 1919 and lost to Jay 10-9 in its first game. Games were popular throughout the years, despite the sheriff stopping Sunday games in 1928. This team is from 1934. The players are, from left to right, as follows: (front row) Ed Whitmire, Tom Mitchell, Golson Harrison, Dub Rivenbark, and McCary; (middle row) Dick Fisher; (back row) Bill Crane, Walton, unknown, John Collis, Snook Stokes, and J.T. Allen.

Minnie Wise Bonifay (standing) and friend played at taking "a tonic" around 1910.

J.W. Urquhart (on right with gun) and friends posed for the camera on Christmas Day, 1910.

Four
Lumber Towns

Just about every town in the county started out as a lumber town to some extent, as small family-run mills dotted every stream. But some towns grew up around a single large mill and became identified with it. Here a group of sawyers pose with their 6-foot long crosscut saws that took two men to push and pull. A large mill usually employed twice as many men in the forests as they did at the mill.

After a tree was cut, it was hauled to the nearest river or railroad by these men and their oxen teams, always led by a white ox. With wheels 8 or 9 feet tall, these "carts" were maneuvered so that the axle was over the tree trunk, which was then winched up off the ground, making it easier to drag.

During the "spring freshet" when the rivers and streams were full, the logs could be floated and/or rafted downstream. Sometimes the logs were attached end to end with "dogs," spikes driven into each end with a short chain between them which enabled the connected logs to be floated down a flume. Such a flume, with logs and dogs can be seen at the Arcadia Historical Park.

Bagdad Land and Lumber Company was the largest landholder in the county, owning over 200,000 acres, much of what is now Blackwater River State Forest. To harvest the timber, the company built the Florida and Alabama Railroad north to Alaflora. Some of the cut trees were 4 feet in diameter. The Pace Mill also had a railroad to Jay.

Bagdad was started when Joseph Forsyth and the Simpson brothers moved the sawmill from Arcadia to the mouth of Pond Creek around 1840, calling the new town Bagdad. It is not known when a post office was established, but it was probably around 1867. Mary Joiner (center) was appointed postmistress in 1896 and served until 1940. Gertrude Gauger was the next postmistress, serving until 1975. After her death, her heirs donated the tiny building to the Bagdad Village Preservation Association.

After Joseph Forsyth died in 1855, the mill was reorganized under E.E. Simpson. From 1866 to 1903, during which time this photo was taken, the mill was known as Simpson and Company. Sold to a Chicago firm, it became Stearns and Culver, and when resold in 1922, Bagdad Land and Lumber Company. It employed almost a thousand men and shipped cut lumber to New Orleans, South America, and Europe. The waterfront was stacked with lumber as far as the eye could see.

Bagdad was very much a company town; the roads and bridges, the commissary, and most of the houses were built by the mill. The power plant not only provided electricity for the mill, but also the town and some of Milton, too. The trees that the early owners thought would last two hundred years were gone in one hundred, and the mill was closed in 1939.

Bagdad had a shipyard as early as 1833, and it was enlarged by William Ollinger and Martin Bruce in 1858. They built the area's first floating drydock that could lift a boat out of the water. It was very successful until the retreating Confederates destroyed the shipyard and burned a nearly completed gunboat being built for the Confederate Navy. The owners sank the drydock themselves to save it.

After the war, the owners rebuilt and raised the drydock. In 1894, Martin Bruce bought out the Ollingers, and the Bruce Drydock continued operations, despite an increasing scarcity of good timber, until 1917. Here, the City of Tampa is in for repairs. Bagdad also had a sash and door factory along the waterfront.

Built between 1858 and 1860 by Benjamin Thompson, one of the mill owners, this house originally faced the river. It was moved in 1912 on log rollers and pulled by mules. When the Northern troops raided Bagdad during the Civil War, they wrote on the walls in charcoal, "Mr. Thompson, Spurling's First Florida Cavalry camped in your house on the 26th of October, 1864." It was discovered by the Clayton and D'Asaro families during their restoration.

The Bagdad Inn was opened on September 22, 1913, by Miss Ahl. It served as a popular place for dinner meetings in addition to serving overnight guests. Located on the corner of Main and Church Streets, the inn was torn down in 1941; only the kitchen, now converted to a house, remains.

Even before the Civil War, Mulat had a ferrry and a mill, which was rebuilt after the Confederates burned it. Simeon Otis bought the mill in 1899 along with a large house built by the previous owner. By 1910, Mulat had a post office, depot, one-room school, church, hotel, company store, and two rows of houses for its sixty employees. "Mr. Simmy" also planted a large satsuma grove. The Crist family is pictured here on their porch. (Photograph courtesy of Special Collections, University of West Florida Library.)

In 1916, Otis launched the new motorized ferry, *The Missing Link*, which held ten autos and crossed to the old Skinner Mill site (by Olive Road today). When the mill closed in 1920 and the ferry stopped in 1926, the town faded. Otis died in 1929, and the entire site was sold to A.G. McMillan in 1938. The buildings decayed and were demolished; only the Duval-Otis-McMillan house remains. (Photo courtesy of Special Collections, University of West Florida Library.)

The Bay Point Mill was reorganized by William Keyser in 1871, but was sold a few years after his death to an Italian consortium. It was run by E. Campodonico and G. Parodi. In 1904, the Rosasco brothers (William, Albert, and Peter) bought the 238 acres of Bay Point and adjacent company town of Pinewood, along with 68,000 acres of timberland. They were already successful timber exporters, owning their own ships that carried cut lumber to Genoa, Italy.

The mill was built out over the water with two wharves for the three-masted schooners that hauled the lumber. The 1917 hurricane destroyed much of the raw timber. Then, after the First World War, international exports declined drastically. Since Bay Point had no railroad access to the interior, the mill declined. It closed in 1919, and the machinery was bought by McGowin and moved to his Milton mill. The Rosascos retained the house and shipyard, which had built a subchaser during the war.

The mill owner's house at Bay Point was built in 1856 by lumberman Edmund Anderson Pearce. Though his "Dover Mill" was burned by retreating Confederates in 1862, the house survived to become the opulent home of William and Harriet Keyser. The house was later the childhood home of author Adelia Rosasco-Soule. Left vacant after World War II, the building was vandalized and burned in 1981.

The small town by the mill was called Pinewood since there already was a Bay Point in the eastern Florida panhandle. It had a post office, a school, and company housing. The houses were moved off the property, but one has been restored by Mr. and Mrs. Gordon Wells.

In 1913, Bagdad Lumber Company built a railroad to Munson to develop the timber, naval stores, and agriculture (on the cut-over lands). C.M. Munson was the manager. From a starting population of four hundred, it grew to one thousand by 1917, the second largest town in the county. The company offices (above), machines shops, and the locomotive roundhouse were located on one side of a wide double street divided by a row of trees.

On the other side of the street were the commissary, school, hotel, theater, church, tennis courts, and a gas station that also sold hamburgers. Every so often, the company declared a day off and everyone went on a picnic. These people waited in front of the commissary for the barbecue to start in 1914.

The rosin yard and storage tanks were near the railroad tracks. A 1926 fire destroyed a double still along with seventy-five barrels of rosin and two carloads of raw gum. The turpentine stills made Bagdad Land and Lumber Company the largest single-operation producer of naval stores in America.

The men of the town took off a day for a political rally. Besides the logging and turpentine stills, the mill started a huge diversified farming operation called the Florida Livestock and Agricultural Farms. In 1917, they had 2,000 head of Hereford cattle, 250 registered Duroc hogs that won prizes in the 1918 State Fair, in addition to 3,200 peach trees, 1,700 grape vines, 700 pecan trees, 65 acres of sweet potatoes, 5 acres of satsuma orange trees and grapefruit.

Munson's Agricultural High School was built in 1924 on 40 acres donated by the lumber company. It was the second largest school in the county, next to Milton's school. Built of brick, it had electric lights and indoor plumbing. The building burned in 1973. This picture was taken in front of the old wooden school in 1921.

By 1931, the town dwindled, as the mill moved its operations north to Alaflora to work the 23,000-acre tract purchased from the Atkinson Lumber Company. It even loaded some of the houses and the Baptist church on flatcars and moved them north. Above is one of the lumber camps, Stearns and Culver Camp No. 8, probably north of Munson, between 1903 and 1912.

In 1935, Congressman Millard Caldwell announced that the federal government would buy huge tracts of cut-over lands, some of which had already been set aside as a state game preserve four years earlier. It necessitated a relocation of six hundred families, out of the fifteen hundred that lived in the northeastern area. Their houses were demolished and the land reforested.

In 1938, Munson became the headquarters for the national forest, which used the old hotel as offices and added warehouses, machine shops, blacksmith shops, new residences, and a 20-acre nursery. Firetowers and fishponds were constructed. When Caldwell became governor, he had the forest transferred to the State, which enabled the local school system to share in the logging profits. The Blackwater River State Forest now encompasses 183,000 acres.

When the 1906 hurricane destroyed Skinner's Mill on Escambia Bay, James G. Pace bought the remains, along with 100,000 acres of timberlands. He moved the machinery to the Floridatown Road, north of the present-day Highway 90 and built the mill, a commissary, workers' housing, and a railroad spur to Jay. By 1912, the area around the mill was referred to as Pace, but was still smaller than Floridatown. The mill employed over two hundred people when it burned in 1925.

Despite dwindling timber supplies, Burgess Pace and James Spencer rebuilt the mill on a smaller scale. It closed permanently around 1928–9, by which time the Paces were already concentrating on farming the cut-over lands. The post office closed in 1925, but growth was facilitated by the Escambia River Bridge, which when built in 1926, routed cars through Pace instead of Floridatown and Mulat.

County prisoners were leased to mill owners and turpentine still operators, who were responsible for their care. The highest bidder in 1917 was the Bagdad Mill, which paid the county $21.75 per month per man, and under a new program, $7.50 per woman. The State stopped this practice in 1924, allowing prisoners only to do county road work. Santa Rosa then leased its convicts to Escambia County's road department.

The Pace home was on Highway 90. In the 1930s, the Pace Brothers had all the houses along the main highway moved so that they could plant tobacco where passing folks could see the new crop that they were touting as an alternative to King Cotton. They built several sheds for curing and drying.

The Pace commissary, located on the northwest side of Floridatown Road and Highway 90, was one of the largest stores in the county. J.G. Pace sold his grocery wholesale business, Consolidated Grocery Company, in 1921. It became the Avant-Pace Company, and when Pace acquired $150,000 in stock in 1930, he changed the name to the Pace Company. It was one of the largest wholesalers in the two county area.

Johnny Hamilton, Dr. Jim Thames (with branding iron), Roland Hamilton, Willy Penton, and the young Rufus Thames (from left to right) brand their free-range cattle on the Thames' and Hamilton's farms in the early 1940s. Every Sunday afternoon, the Hamiltons butchered a cow to take to the commissary on Monday morning. In 1928, Santa Rosa County had seven thousand head of cattle, mainly Hereford—preferred by the Pace and Munson Farms. The Pace Farm also had a large number of Duroc hogs.

Henry Penton was the chief lumber grader at the mill and carried lumber home each day to build his house near the northeast corner of Floridatown Road and Highway 90. This photo is from the 1940s before the restoration done by his son, Pace historian Frank Penton.

Penton's Grocery and Market was on Highway 90. Frank is seen here with his parents. In 1936, it was robbed by two men with guns and a female getaway driver. Although Henry Penton fired three shots as the car fled toward Pensacola, the trio escaped with $135.

The Penton Town School, north of Pace, was open from 1890 to 1930. It was a two-room frame building with separate doors, one for girls and one for boys. The man on the far right is John Diamond, county school superintendent from 1912 to 1916. Promoting consolidation, he visited every one of the sixty white and nine black schools. By 1923, Santa Rosa County led the state in school consolidation.

During the term of School Superintendent Raymond Hobbs, the construction of consolidated and brick schools was accelerated. Between 1924 and 1926, the Harold, McLellan, Wallace, and Pace Schools were built using the same basic plan. These Pace teachers probably taught two grades each in 1926. Students went to high school in Milton until the seventies, when Pace High was built.

When M. Fillmore Adams came to Pace to farm around 1900, sugar cane was a big crop. He started a cane mill to produce syrup, which was continued by his son, Millard Adams Sr., when he returned from the service. He continued to grind the cane, extracting the juice, and then cooking it into syrup "the old way," with the help of his three sons, until the twin hurricanes of 1995 destroyed the equipment.

Concurrent with the 1920s land boom was the satsuma orange craze. Thousands of trees were planted by the Pace and Munson Farms, by Sim Otis in Mulat, and by the Porter Interests in Holt. A hard freeze of 12 degrees on February 5, 1924, slowed it down somewhat, although a 1930 brochure still touted Santa Rosa as ideal for satsumas. Also popular in the thirties were tung nut trees, raised for their oil.

Five
Other Towns

Andrew Jackson was believed to have camped at Floridatown and crossed the bay here. Floridatown was an important town, for both the ferry and for fun. It remained a popular resort into the fifties.

The Floridatown ferry was a major link to Pensacola even in the 1800s. In 1916, the *Freshwater* held eight autos and crossed over to Ferry Pass three times a day, each trip taking thirty minutes. Despite building a new wharf, dredging out the sandbar, changing the landing site to a clay road, and adding an engine, it was eclipsed by the Mulat ferry. By 1919, the ferry landed in Mulat, and by 1926, when the bridge was built, it was moved to a Town Point (Gulf Breeze) and Pensacola run.

The pier and cottages at Floridatown were popular attractions even before the Floridatown pavilion was built in 1926. It replaced the large cottage at the land end of the pier. Several of the cottages were also torn down when the Allen Hotel was built in the early twenties.

A.P. Hardee built the Bayview Hotel in 1912. In 1915, indoor bathrooms were added. He sold it to the Rollo Brothers in June 1925, who then sold it to the Pace Brothers the following month. The Pace Brothers added a dancing pavilion, remodeled the hotel, and renamed it the Merry Gardens Hotel. The Pace family carried on the tradition that had started in the 1800s of having huge Fourth of July celebrations here with free fish fries. The opening of the new courthouse and Escambia River Bridge were also cause for celebrations here. It was at one such event in 1936 that they announced the "grand opening" of the renamed Jackson Hotel and Andrew Jackson pavilion. They added a swimming pool the following year. It continued its popularity until Navarre Beach was opened up with the bridge in 1960. The hotel was torn down in 1968.

R.J. Allen built a dancing pavilion here between 1920 and 1922, but the Satsuma Pavilion was destroyed in the 1926 hurricane. That same year, the Pace Brothers built the 70' x 135' Merry Gardens Pavilion. Governor John Martin was here to open the celebratory ball. The pavilion was knocked off its foundation in the same hurricane. In 1936, it was renamed the Andrew Jackson Pavilion.

Dances were held here three times a week with live bands, often from New Orleans. The floor had lights implanted in it that shone upward. Sometimes the crowds got a little rowdy, such as the time they shot out the lights in 1927. An injunction to close the place down for drinking and disorderly conduct was denied by Judge Thomas West, but the pavilion closed for a while anyway, for repairs.

In 1919, Milton entrepreneur, R.J. Allen bought an entire block of cottages at Floridatown with plans to build a "pleasure resort." Shortly thereafter, he opened the Allen, a hotel that specialized in weekend parties and Sunday dinners. It had electric lights and indoor bathrooms. In 1923, R.J. Allen sold the hotel and Satsuma pavilion to a Chicago developer, Czaja's, who renamed it the Satsuma Beach Inn.

This is an unknown house at Floridatown.

The 1920s were a time of rampant land speculation by Northern investors. Huge tracts of land changed hands frequently, and several new real estate firms sprang up to handle the business. One such land deal was Floridale, and another was Avalon Beach. Bought in 1925 by Chicago speculators, the land was divided into twenty thousand lots that were advertised as "high and dry." This advertisement is from the fifties.

The ad also stated that many beautiful homes had already been completed, that a post office and "First Church" were open, that a bridge across Del Monte (Mulatto) Bayou was under construction, and that roads were being paved. The majority of the land is still owned by Lake Shore Realty in Chicago.

Chumuckla Springs was a popular resort in 1912, with a forty-room hotel and several guest cottages. Reached by launch from McDavid and later by bridges, the spring provided curative mineral waters for drinking and bathing. The hotel burned in 1915, injuring Drs. Bryan and Barker when they jumped from a second-floor window. Although a few cabins were built over the years by different owners, it never regained its popularity. The post office that had opened in 1914 was closed in 1920.

The mineral water was piped across the river to McDavid, where it was bottled in half-gallon jugs and five-gallon demijohns. The water had been deemed particularly beneficial for pellagra, a disease characterized by burning dermatitis, diarrhea, and dementia. The hotel meals probably did more good than the water, as pellagra was discovered in 1915 to be the result of a dietary deficiency. The water was still being bottled and shipped as far away as Chicago in the thirties.

Chumuckla became a farming area as the trees were cut by the Pace mill which owned 97,000 acres in the area. The Pace Farms, under Burgess Pace and Joe Jernigan, promoted scientific farming. Cotton was the major crop despite warnings as early as 1917 to cut production. When the price of cotton fell drastically, Pace Farms started growing tobacco. They also had large satsuma groves. This is the Joel McDavid farmhouse between Chumuckla and Coon Hill.

Smaller independent farmers, as well as the Pace Farms, had herds of Hereford cattle and also raised Duroc hogs. Corn and hay were needed for feed. This hay wagon was on the Joel McDavid farm.

The Pace Brothers put in a cotton gin and feed mill in Chumuckla in 1924. At first a steam plant, it was later converted to diesel. It had two Munger System Pratt Continental eight-saw gins, complete with double box revolving press with automatic packer. It had a capacity of thirty bales a day. It also had a Williams pulverizer, feed crusher, corn shucker, sheller and grinder, oat and chop crusher, and pea sheller. It was open to the public on Wednesdays and Saturdays at reasonable rates. The commissary is on the left.

In 1939, a new Murray gin was installed along with a feed mill featuring the latest crushing and mixing equipment. Pace Farms produced their own brand of feed, Pacemaker. They also had a 3,000-gallon tank for blackstrap molasses for producing sweet feeds. Jay, too, had a gin, installed in 1922, and Milton had one built by the railroad tracks in northern Milton in 1928. Milton had had a gin by the depot at the turn of the century, but it had been closed for several years.

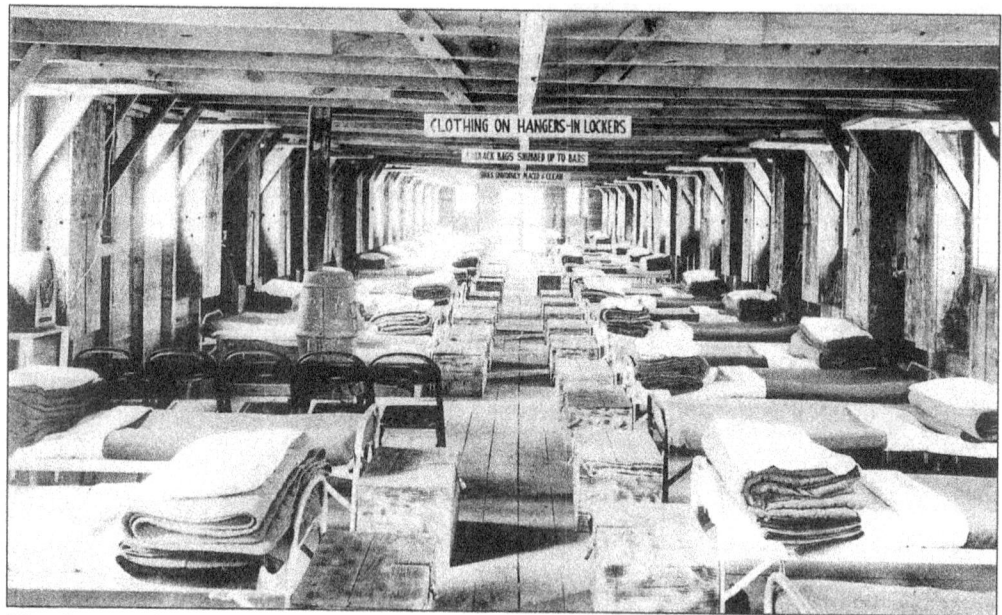

The first Civilian Conservation Corps (CCC) Camp in Milton's area was Metts Tower in Okaloosa County. Two hundred forty-six local young men were enrolled in the physically demanding work of building bridges and clearing roads and firebreaks in the forests. A second camp was started in Chumuckla, on the Pace property, in 1934. They were run like army camps, with a commanding officer, a superintendent, and a few expert tractor operators. In 1935, the Chumuckla camp was converted to a CCC camp for young black men.

McLellan was named for the McLellan family; one of whom, John L., was elected sheriff in 1863. John Temple built a commissary to serve the needs of the several turpentine and logging camps in the area. He also had a turpentine still and twenty-five to thirty tenant houses for workers and farmers. In 1927, he built a new store with timber he cut himself. "McLellan" was painted on the roof for the Whiting pilots. It closed around 1978.

Allentown was named for one of its earliest settlers, Jessie Carter Allen, who was also the county's first sheriff (1842–5). Because of its proximity to the big mills, it was one of the first cut-over areas and thus the first major agricultural area. Ben Jernigan, another early settler, had a small sawmill on Clear Creek. James Jernigan is seen here resting in front of his farmhouse in Allentown in 1903.

Jessie Carter Allen raised sheep in Allentown as did many other farmers. It was ideal for cut-over lands because no stump removal was needed. In 1930, Santa Rosa County had fifty thousand sheep, more than any other county in Florida, and produced over 100,000 pounds of wool yearly. This photo is dated 1907. Sheep-raising had declined even before the open ranges were fenced in 1949.

In 1917, the Allentown livestock breeders formed an association to decide on breeds, choosing Red-Polled cattle and Duroc hogs. That same year, they put in the first county vat for dipping cattle for ticks. (Munson and Pace Farms had their own.) The county was declared tick free ten years later, after the State built sixty vats. In 1928, they organized a Bull Association to purchase registered bulls, in this case for Jersey dairy cows.

The nucleus of Allentown is the Farm Center, which buys and sells peanuts, wheat, oats, and other grains. They are graded, cleaned, dried, bagged, stacked on ton pallets, and shipped out. Before the 1995 hurricanes, Erin and Opal, destroyed the drying bin, the center also handled soybeans.

Allentown had a couple of schools that were consolidated into the new brick school in 1923. It was built by the local people with bricks they made in Allentown. It was the first agricultural high school, although it only went through the tenth grade. The Hammock Pond School near the crossroads was closed. The county's first school buses were built by Luther King and his father. This bus was driven by Alvin Spurlock around 1923.

According to the 1930 census, Allentown showed the greatest increase in population, from 61 to 492. Mr. Barker built a general store on the northwest corner of the crossroads to accommodate their needs in the thirties. It was rebuilt by Willie Ware in 1946 and is now owned by Morris Ward.

A pig and some chickens foraged in an unidentified barnyard around 1910–15. Poultry was another important farm product, the largest producer in the twenties being the Kea-Ring Farm in Floridale. Owned by R.T. Ringling and Dr. George Keally, this farm had over five thousand hens and sold both eggs (1,800 a day) and broilers. Smaller farmers were dependent on wholesalers such as W.C. Salter, who started in 1916 with one truck and ten years later covered a two-county area.

In the boom years of the twenties, Santa Rosa was touted as the fruit belt where even peaches, apples, and cherries grew well. Many acres were also planted with grapes, such as these on the W.W. Harrison farm in Harold. One of the first grape enthusiasts was James Ouzoonian who bought 2,400 acres, planted grapes, and shipped out the first carload in 1928. J. Frank Smith started out in 1924 with mainly a sweet-native variety, Maiden Blush. By 1930, he had 1,000 acres in grapes and shipped them all over the country.

Francis Augustus Harrison played with piglets on his father's farm in Harold around 1909. Originally called Good Range, the town was renamed for Harold Porter, whose father had huge land holdings in the area. Porter planned to rename Holt after his other son, Huston, but the townsfolk refused to change.

At the first snap of cold weather, hogs were slaughtered and put into the smokehouse to cure. The ice plant in Milton would do this for the city folk starting in 1931. Jay got an ice plant and cold storage in 1945.

Mules and donkeys were the main source of power on the farm. In 1918, the B.M. Jernigan farm in Jay is described by the *Milton Gazette* as a "four-mule farm" (one mule was needed for every 40 acres). Donkeys were also used for entertainment, for donkey baseball games were popular in 1936. Tom Golson (center front), W.W. Powell (on donkey), and Frank Harrison (on right) got this donkey to stand still for this *c*. 1905 photograph.

This early piece of farm equipment was pulled by a mule. Farmers started plowing the ground for spring planting after Christmas, since it was so slow and laborious. Although Fordson tractors were demonstrated by the Allen-Faircloth Motor Company as early as 1922, they remained rare, used mainly to remove stumps.

According to tradition, Jay took its name from the first store owner in town, J.T. Nowling. The post office was located in his building in 1902. Jay was incorporated in 1904. Wiley Cannon was the mayor.

This is a livery stable in Jay in the early 1900s.

Harrison Mercantile Company, built in 1917, was Jay's first large commercial establishment. The post office was moved to the brick store. It had a small fire in 1936, but the mail was saved. Harrison's was the only store in Jay that did not close during the Depression.

In 1922, Harrison Mercantile Company added a cotton gin, the only one in Santa Rosa at the time. By 1926, it was ginning a bale of cotton every twenty minutes, day and night. Santa Rosa was the second largest cotton-producing county in the state in 1930. Farmers got a half to three-quarters of a bale an acre.

In 1917, Jay had a six-room frame schoolhouse that was second in size to Milton's school. A brick school for grades one through twelve that consolidated the Cora, Mt. Carmel, Pine Level, and Ebenezer Schools was built in 1926. With eight hundred students, it was the largest rural school in Florida. In 1933, the school burned but was quickly rebuilt with the help of a $100,000 CWA grant.

Poor roads isolated Jay from Milton and encouraged closer association to nearby Alabama towns. When the County ran out of money to gravel the Flomaton Road in 1922, seventy-five men came with twenty-six teams of mules to spend a day spreading a mile of gravel. In December 1930, the County finally surveyed a new road from Milton, straightening kinks and eliminating wet spots. It was paved in 1937. This Clee-track machine worked on a road outside of Jay in 1923.

Jay had a building boom in 1939, when four new brick businesses were added, one of which was the Santa Rosa Theater. The Rural Electrification Administration (REA) opened a headquarters in the Kent building, and the State built a huge livestock market. The market opened in October 1940, and by January 1950, it was selling $100,000 worth of livestock a month. In 1946, two peanut warehouses also opened.

A windmill on an unknown farm in Jay pumped water from the well. In the seventies, the Jay skyline was dotted with a different kind of derrick because oil was discovered and many wells drilled.

In 1930, A.J. Beland colonized 30,000 acres of cut-over lands 6 miles northeast of Munson. It was first called St. Lumina and later Santa Maria, but is remembered as Belandville. By 1933, the five hundred French-speaking Northerners had a post office, Catholic church, cannery, creamery, and brick hardware store.

The colonists cleared the land of stumps and planted eighteen thousand strawberry plants and other fruits and vegetables. Their success at growing was stymied by a lack of accessible markets and poor transportation. The town declined in the late thirties and the people moved away. The houses were moved to Munson, the church was dismantled with parts being used elsewhere, and the graves were moved to St. Michael's Cemetery in Pensacola.

Around 1900, a consortium known as the Porter Interests bought 50,000 acres around Holt and planted satsumas, peaches, pecans, grapes, and vegetables. R.T. Ringling and W.L. White bought the property with plans to start a new town. To attract Northerners, they built the sixty-room Hotel Granda in 1927. Designed by John Stafford White, it was a Spanish-style structure with white stucco, blue trim, and a red tile roof. This building housed the bell and water towers and hydroelectric plant. The completely furnished hotel never opened. Built at a cost of $150,000, it was sold for $20,000 at foreclosure in 1932. It was stripped of salvageable materials in 1943 and torn down. The towers remained until 1968. As is the case of so many places seen in this book, nothing now remains but a memory and a photo, both of which fade with time.

www.ingramcontent.com/pod-product-compliance
Lightning Source LLC
Chambersburg PA
CBHW080906100426
42812CB00007B/2185